Mapping in the Modern World

MAPPING THE FUTURE

James Bow

Crabtree Publishing Company
www.crabtreebooks.com

Crabtree Publishing Company
www.crabtreebooks.com
1-800-387-7650

Published in Canada
616 Welland Ave.
St. Catharines, ON
L2M 5V6

Published in the United States
PMB 59051
350 Fifth Ave. 59th Floor
New York, NY 10118

Published in 2017 by CRABTREE PUBLISHING COMPANY

Author: James Bow

Managing Editor: Tim Cooke

Designer: Melissa Roskell

Cover Design: Katherine Berti

Picture Manager: Sophie Mortimer

Design Manager: Keith Davis

Editorial Director: Lindsey Lowe, Kathy Middleton

Editor: Janine Deschenes

Children's Publisher: Anne O'Daly

Proofreader: Ellen Rodger

Production coordinator and Prepress technician: Ken Wright

Print coordinator: Margaret Amy Salter

Produced by Brown Bear Books for
Crabtree Publishing Company

Photo credits

Photographs (t=top, b=bottom, l=left, r=right, c=center)

Front Cover: Wikimedia Commons: inset first, third, and fouth from left; All other images from Shutterstock

Interior: CERN: 27; Denis Wood: 25; ESA/NASA: 28c; Google Inc.: 18, Google Earth 28b, Google Maps 8b; HYPERLINK "http://www.arizonaroads.com" www.arizonaroads.com: 16bl, HYPERLINK "http://www.elpasoco.com" www.elpasoco.com: 22/23; SA1 Geography 29b; HYPERLINK "http://www.vidiani.com" www.vidiani.com: 16br.;NASA: 10, 11, 13, 14, 24: NOAA: 12, 15, 26, 29t; Public Domain: 29c; Oliver O'Brien: 17; Open Street Map: 8t; Shutterstock: Alexey Boldin 9, George JMC Little 23b, Tyler Olson 7, Roman Pyshchyk 6b, Ymgerman 9; U.S. Census Bureau: 20; Washington Post: 21.
All other photos, artwork and maps, Brown Bear Books.

Brown Bear Books has made every attempt to contact the copyright holder. If you have any information please contact licensing@brownbearbooks.co.uk

Library and Archives Canada Cataloguing in Publication

Bow, James, 1972-, author
Mapping the future / James Bow.

(Mapping in the modern world)
Includes index.
Issued in print and electronic formats.
ISBN 978-0-7787-3238-9 (hardcover).--
ISBN 978-0-7787-3244-0 (softcover).--
ISBN 978-1-4271-1887-5 (HTML)

1. Cartography--Juvenile literature. 2. Cartography--Technological innovations--Juvenile literature. 3. Cartography--Forecasting--Juvenile literature. I. Title.

GA105.6.B688 2017 j526 C2016-907135-9
C2016-907136-7

Library of Congress Cataloging-in-Publication Data

CIP available at the Library of Congress

Printed in Canada/122021/CPC20211206

Contents

PERSONALIZING MAPS

Advances in technology have changed how people use maps. Individual users can create maps that show the specific information they need at any time.

In the past, maps were physical items. They were drawn or printed, usually on paper, and published for people to buy. Many people bought and used a copy of the same map, even if they all used it for a different purpose. Information that was useful to a car driver might not be useful to someone walking in the wilderness, for example. The driver

Since they appeared in 2014, smartwatches have allowed users to view maps that match their exact location.

might want the map only to examine the roads. A hiker would use the map to look at hiking trails or geographical features.

Most new maps are **digital**. They are created and stored on computers. That makes them far easier to change or update than maps on printed paper. It is also possible for people to **customize** maps to show exactly the information they want in whatever location they happen to be in.

Satellite TecÙology

One of the key steps in making digital maps possible was the use of **satellites**. In 1959, the United States launched Transit. This system of satellites orbited Earth. It used **triangulation** to pinpoint the location of United States Navy ships around the world. By 1993, the United States had 24 satellites orbiting at around 12,600 miles (20,277 km) above the Earth. The satellites could accurately map any point on Earth's surface.

This view of the world at night was created by NASA's Suomi satellite. The main lights show areas that are more densely populated..

In the Real World

A Question of Privacy

As digital maps become more accurate, people are worried about their effects. Google Street View shows people 360-degree photographs of points within Google Maps. The images are taken by Google Street View cars and bikes. They show people what places look like. But Street View cameras also capture people around their neighborhoods, often without their knowledge. The images are then posted online, and become a permanent record. Some people see Google Street View as an invasion of privacy.

Anyone can be photographed by Google Street View and displayed in the online map.

In 1995, the first **Global Positioning System** (GPS) devices went on sale to the public. Now anyone could use satellites to find their location. Mapping software in cars used satellite data to figure out the best routes people could drive. By 2010, GPS devices were small enough to fit inside cell phones. That made it possible for anyone with a cell phone to find the way to any location. On the other hand, the cell phone also tracked the movements of the user.

Cell phones show drivers the best route to a destination. They can also highlight real-time delays along the way.

Using GPS

GPS lies at the heart of many new mapping technologies. It helps hikers keep on the right path and tells sailors and pilots if they are on the correct route. It allows runners or cyclists to map their routes, record their times, and share them with friends. Navigation systems in cars "speak" to drivers to tell them which roads to take. These systems are far safer than reading a paper map while driving. GPS even helps drivers avoid traffic jams up ahead.

GPS is also the basis of a new kind of pastime. It guides people on real-world treasure-hunts, in a hobby called geocaching. When people reach their goal, they discover a "**geocache**." The geocache might be a puzzle to solve or a logbook to sign. Meanwhile, GPS provides important data for scientists to study **climate change** and pollution. The technology is helping scientists to better understand the planet.

Maps and Me

Customized Maps

In the past, mapmakers could only put limited information on maps. They had to choose the information they thought would be useful. Thanks to **Geographic Information Systems** (GIS), a range of data can now be collected virtually anywhere on Earth. Users can use the data to create detailed maps, printing only the information they need. Think about the data you would put on a map for a specific task. For example, if you were looking for lost ruins in the jungle, you might want to examine any unusually shaped lumps in the ground.

New mapping technology is the basis of modern forms of treasure hunting where people use satellite data to find hidden locations.

Breakthroughs

The OpenStreetMap Project

The OpenStreetMap project was created by people who wanted to make maps more widely available. They used public data and local knowledge to build maps of the world full of detail. Unlike Google Street View, the maps are not protected by copyright. That means anyone can print and use them. Thousands of users contribute their own knowledge to the project. They add details of local businesses, footpaths, and other things that are unique to the area. The many pieces of information create a powerful database. Anyone can join the community, and users help answer any questions new users might have.

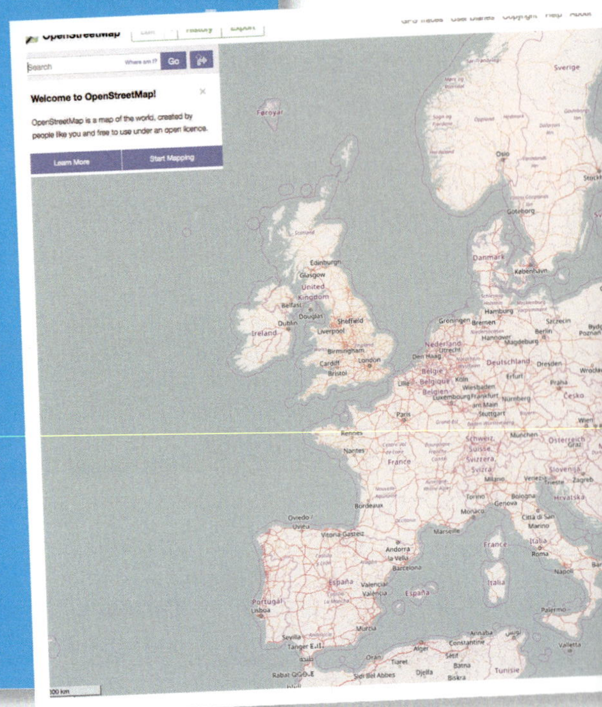

The OpenStreetMap Project aims to make personal, detailed maps available to everyone free of charge.

Negative Effects

Not all the effects of GPS are positive. Technology intended to help people find their way has sometimes had the opposite result. Some people get so used to GPS that they can no longer read traditional maps. Drivers following navigation systems rather than paying attention to their surroundings have turned off roads into fields or lakes due to GPS errors. If people become too reliant on technology, they do not always know how to cope when it breaks down.

Google Earth agreed to requests by the U.S. military to blur military bases and other facilities.

Satellite maps are not only flat. Three-dimensional maps allow users to alter the angle of viewing and to zoom in on particular locations.

Censorship?

The use of satellite technology also raises questions about privacy. Satellites see everything, from military bases to backyards. As part of its Google Earth project, Google has photographed every part of Earth. The United States military asked Google to blur satellite images of its military bases (see page 8). Critics of this blurring accuse Google of **censorship**. They believe that blurring certain images might hide the damage some businesses or governments are doing to the environment.

Maps and Privacy

Apple, meanwhile, got into trouble when it was discovered that its smartphones were monitoring users' locations. Apple was putting them on a map. This raised serious questions about privacy. What if the information got into the wrong hands? Could robbers, for example, learn when homes were empty because their owners were absent? What rights do people have when they use GPS? Should people be allowed to see into other people's backyards? Is new map technology worth the loss of our personal privacy?

Did You Know?

In 2011 it was revealed that Apple was monitoring the location of people as they used their phones. Many people protested at what they said was an invasion of privacy. Apple said it only used the data to improve its services.

FUTURE OF THE ENVIRONMENT

On December 7, 1972, the crew of Apollo 17 took a picture of Earth known as "The Blue Marble." The image became one of the most widely seen pictures in history.

The Blue Marble picture became a symbol of the environmental campaigns of the 1970s. Although it is a photograph, it did what all important maps do. It reminded people of where they are. For many viewers, it was a reminder that everyone shares the same planet. The lesson of the image was that everyone has a responsibility to take care of Earth.

The "Blue Marble" was taken when the Sun was behind the spacecraft. That is why the whole disk of the Earth is lit up clearly.

Seeing the Unseen

One way that maps help experts to understand the environment is by showing things that are not visible to the eye. Today, more than 1,000 active satellites are circling Earth. They can collect data that human **cartographers** cannot. Using devices like **spectrometers**, satellites observe the world through **infrared** and **ultraviolet** lenses that reveal changes in heat. Satellites measure temperature differences

This satellite photo shows Hurricane Matthew, which struck Haiti and parts of the southeast United States in fall 2016.

in the oceans or in the **atmosphere**. This helps scientists monitor the movement of clouds or ocean currents, which enables them to map Earth's climate. Weather satellites are used to track hurricanes. The data are used to generate maps that help **meteorologists** predict the path of the storm. People in danger can then be warned or evacuated. Similar satellites can measure levels of pollution, dust, and smoke in the air.

Understanding Earth's Systems

Satellite pictures can reveal how expanding cities are consuming farmland or how farms are consuming the Amazon rain forest. They help us see and understand how humans are impacting their environment.

Satellites also allow cartographers to help geologists look inside Earth. Sound waves from explosions or earthquakes are recorded by satellites as they travel beneath Earth's surface. **Sonar** and **seismic** readings can help experts measure **aquifers** deep underground to see how much water they contain. The same method can be used to locate oil. Satellites can even map underground changes that warn scientists when a volcano is about to erupt.

Public Access

The Internet has had an important role to play in digital mapping. The Internet puts satellite data in the hands of the public. Anyone can now follow environmental changes for themselves through

This map shows where and when the rubber ducks came ashore (red) and the major currents of the world's oceans (blue).

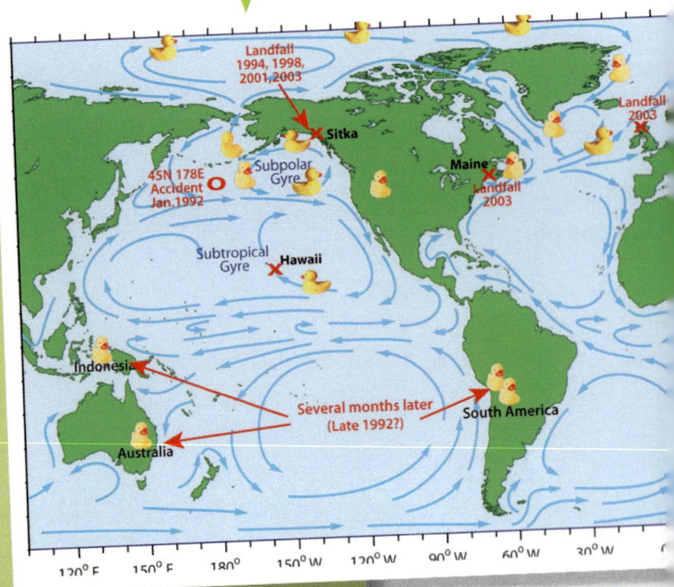

In the Real World

The Rubber Duck Map

Cartographers use maps to track pollution in many ways—even with the help of rubber ducks. In 1992, a ship in the North Pacific Ocean lost a container in a storm. The container released 28,000 plastic ducks into the ocean. Floating ducks washed up 10 months later on the coast of Alaska, 2,000 miles (3,200 km) away. Oceanographers asked people to report the sightings of any more ducks. Between 2004 and 2007, rubber ducks washed up in New England and Great Britain. Oceanographers used the findings to map the ocean currents. The ducks also served to highlight the problem of floating garbage in the oceans.

projects such as NASA's Earth Observatory. The Earth Observatory shares discoveries about Earth from NASA's satellites with the public.

Environment and Climate Change Canada has interactive maps showing a range of environmental indicators. People can use the maps to see what is happening in the whole country or to look up maps showing local air quality and the levels of different types of pollution.

This is a satellite image of India. It uses infrared imaging to show fires lit by farmers to clear fields (red). Smoke from such fires causes pollution.

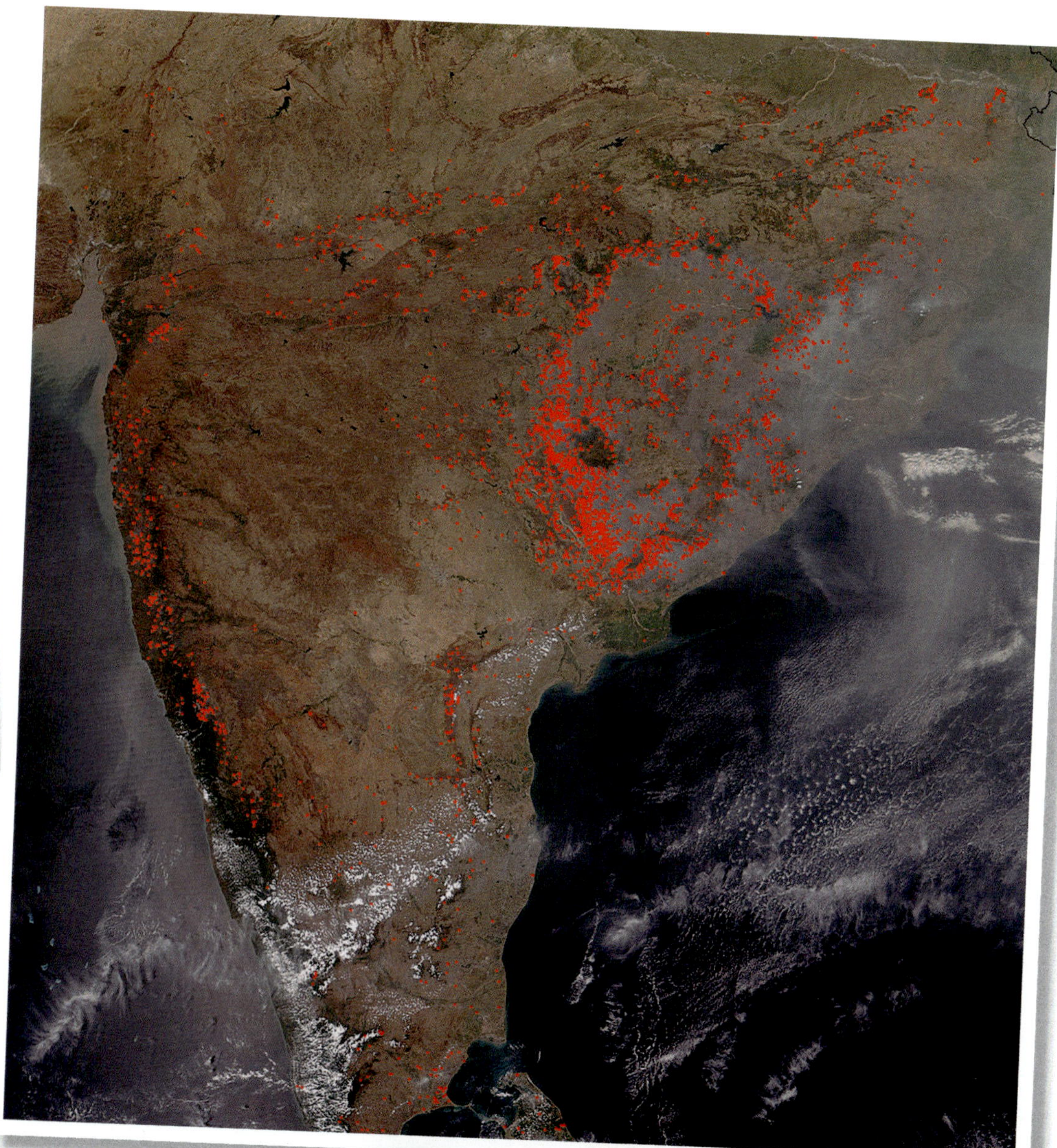

In the Real World

Impact of Cities

Urban sprawl is the name used to describe how growing cities gradually spread into neighboring rural, or countryside, land. Traditional city maps show how much the city has expanded. Satellite photographs can show not only how much cities have grown, but also how much green land, such as trees, wetlands, and fields, have been paved over. Mapping data from satellites also shows changes to water quality and erosion, which developers might not have considered before they start building. TecŸology helps city planners to understand the landscape around them. It shows where they can build and what areas they should avoid.

Green blocks in the center of this image show how the city of Las Vegas is gradually spreading through the dry valleys of Nevada.

Many cell phones already have weather apps that can send weather alerts to users in specific locations. In some regions, these apps even communicate tornado warnings. This data has saved many lives.

Mapping Threats

Maps are one of the first lines of defense against threats to the environment. People who protest against the construction of a new highway might draw its proposed route on a detailed map of local vegetation. That will help to reveal whether the highway might harm sensitive environmental areas. Governments can control levels of urban sprawl by drawing up maps of "green belts." These are areas around a city where construction of homes or industry is not allowed. This all helps to look after the future of the environment.

Did You Know?

Most experts agree that human activity is causing the world to heat up. They warn that this is leading to the melting of the ice caps, which causes a rise in sea levels that will flood coasts and destroy some islands.

Climate Change

The global climate is changing. That makes it more important than ever before to understand environmental change. Satellite maps measure the melting ice caps at the poles. They help predict how much sea levels could rise as a result of melting ice. **Climatologists** also use maps to predict how weather patterns will change, and how that will affect people. Mapping technology can reveal the planet in the past as well as in the future. Looking at past environmental changes and weather patterns can help scientists to predict what will happen—and to do something about it.

This map shows the extent of the Arctic ice cap (white) in summer in 1885 and 1995, with a prediction of how it may appear in summer 2085 if global warming continues at its current rate.

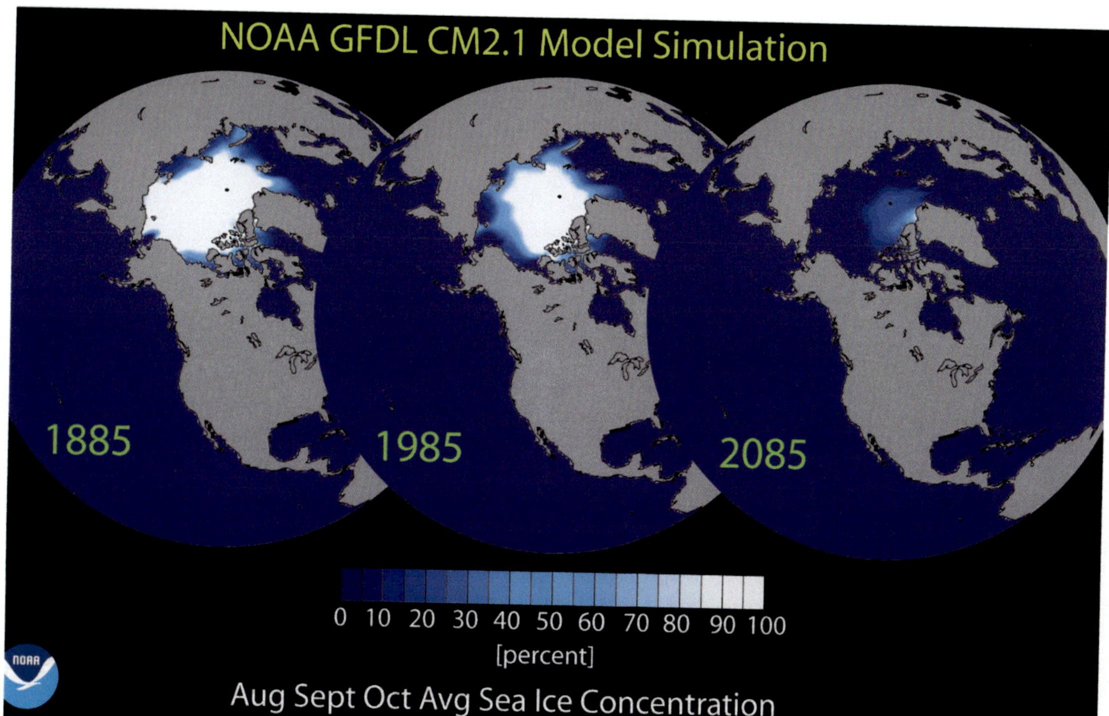

FUTURE OF TRAVEL

The invention of new transportation methods means that more people are traveling further than ever before. Mapping technology helps us all find our way around.

In the 1800s, the invention of the bicycle, railroads, and the automobile enabled more people to travel more widely. In the 1920s and 1930s, tire manufacturers and gas companies wanted to encourage more people to travel in the United States. These companies gave away millions of road maps. The maps showed key routes, and the location of gas stations, diners, and lodging. These maps encouraged drivers to explore the country.

Interactive Driving

In the early 2000s, GPS systems began to be used in cars. They gave drivers turn-by-turn directions to their destination. The maps on these systems often featured details of local businesses, such as restaurants, stores, and hotels.

These automobile maps of New Mexico show how the road network has changed over 80 years as different highways become more or less important.

2012

1927

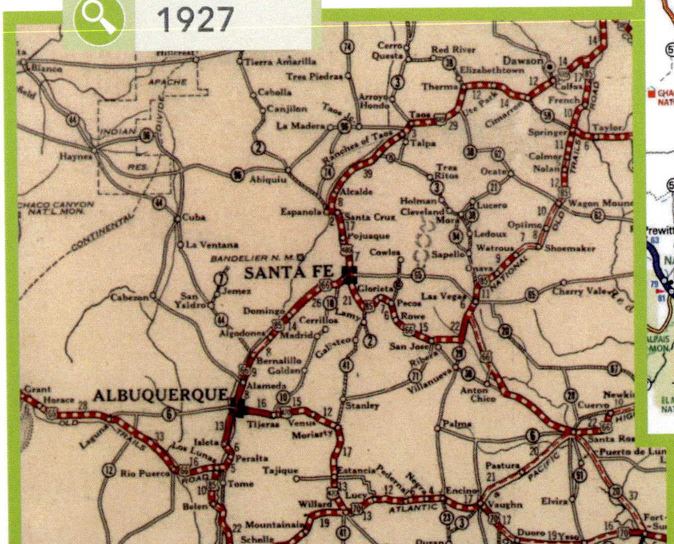

Maps and Me

Dude, Where's My Bike?

Online maps can be updated instantly. That makes them useful for travel. They are used by community bike and car-share programs, which have bikes or cars around cities for use by their members. Maps tell users what bikes and cars are available to rent nearby. Any data coded with location information can be used to make maps. Why not try making your own real-time map? You could map the school parking lot. Use colored pencils to show full and empty spaces over an hour or two. Use an eraser to update your map. Is there a pattern of where spaces are used most?

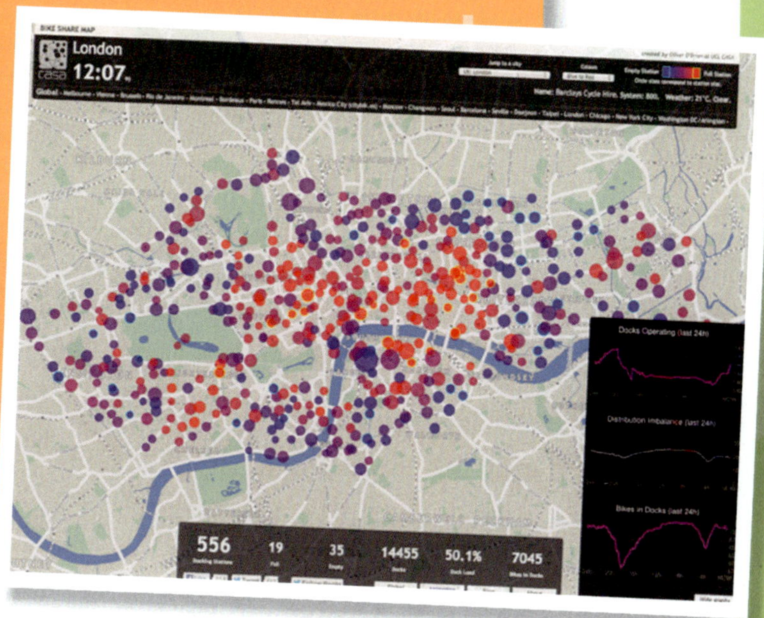

This London community cycle program map shows real-time data about where to find and park rental bikes.

GPS systems are still being improved. They give users instant notification of wrecks or roadworks, plan alternate routes, and estimate the length of time the new journey will take.

Self-Driving Cars

Many companies such as Google, Tesla, and Uber are developing self-driving cars. Self driving vehicles use GPS and robotics technology that allow them to "learn" and follow maps. Some people worry about what might happen if the computer systems break down. Self-driving cars may also put truck drivers and other transportation workers out of work.

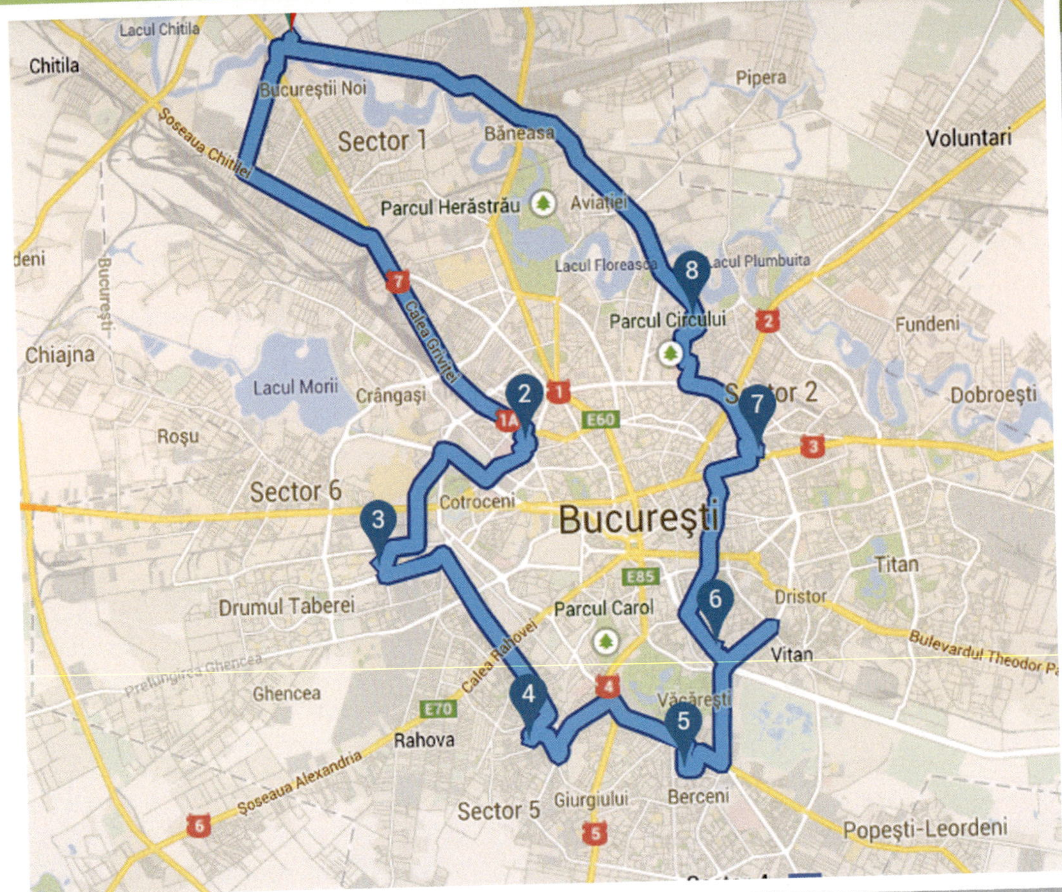

This map shows a delivery route around Bucharest in Romania. Each stop is numbered in order.

Delivery Systems

GPS data and computers help many businesses plan things such as operations and deliveries. Many people shop online and have their purchases delivered to their homes. Delivery businesses use mapping technology to calculate the most efficient routes for their drivers. This saves time and enables the drivers to make more deliveries.

Computer programs figure out the best routes for each driver. Using GPS information from individual vehicles, the program can even change routes when the driver is on the road. It can accommodate a new pick-up address, for example, or help drivers avoid roadworks or slow-moving traffic.

Did You Know?

There are many stories of GPS errors. In one case a driver from Syria drove to the village of Gibraltar in Scotland rather than Gibraltar, a British territory on Spain's south coast. The two locations are 1,600 miles (2,575 km) apart.

Other Transportation

Mapping technology is not only changing road travel. Passengers on airplanes have been able to follow their journey on a sky map for decades. Now, friends or relatives can also watch their progress on a flight tracker website. Pedestrians can plan routes using mapping apps that direct them away from areas with pollution. Users of public transportation can learn the precise position of a bus and when it will reach a stop. In some systems, mapping apps even tell users how much room there is on the bus.

The Uber app shows users what cars are in their neighborhood and where they are on their journey.

In the Real World

The Uber Economy

In the mid-2000s, the combination of smart phones and GPS systems was used to create Uber, Lyft, and other taxi companies. GPS systems picked the fastest routes and the phones figured out the cost of the ride. The GPS system meant that drivers did not need to know an area in order to reach a destination. Some people worry that new tecŸology will impact people's ability to navigate for themselves. Scientists believe that when people memorize things such as driving routes, part of their brain grows larger. This part of the brain specializes in navigation. Relying on GPS systems may make that part of the brain weaker.

FUTURE OF PLANNING

One important role of maps is to help people prepare for the future. As world populations grow, mapping human behavior becomes more crucial.

Planners use maps and computer programs to predict the effects of various changes on neighborhoods and their residents. Changes such as a growing or falling population, an increase in the average age of a population, or a rise in the number of families with small children might all require action by local or national planners. Such changes could include building new retirement homes or schools, for example. Authorities might also redraw the boundaries of political districts to ensure that their populations are largely equal.

The U.S. National Census allows users to generate their own interactive maps of a region or the whole country, showing data of their choice. Details are on page 31.

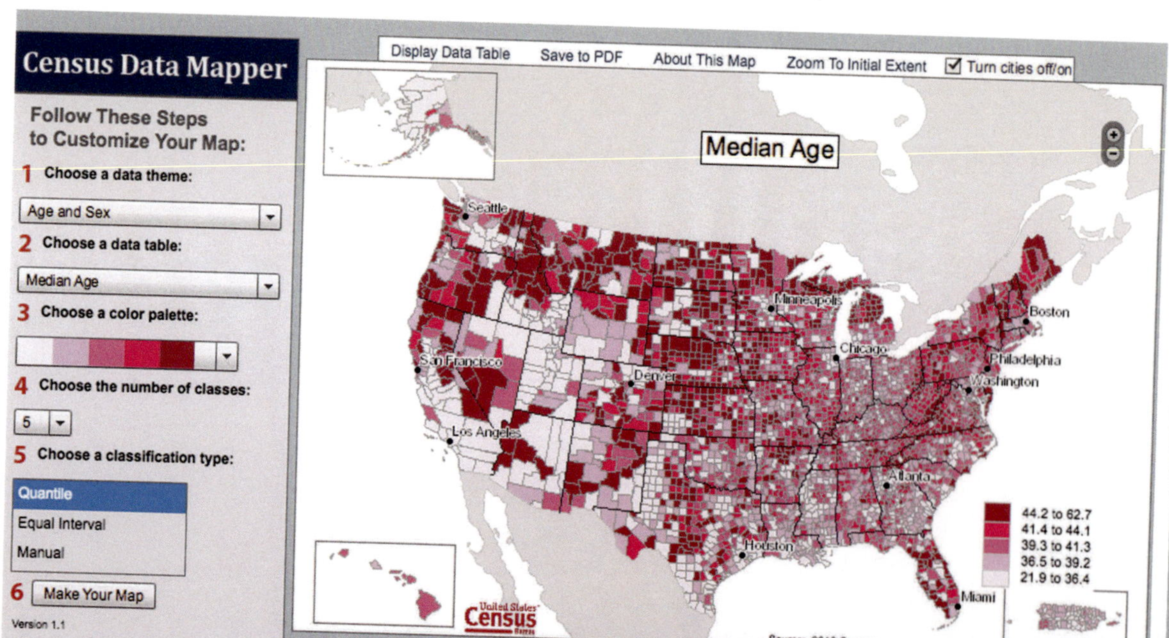

In the Real World

Playing with Boundaries

One change that is led by mapping is redrawing the boundaries of political districts. In some states, political parties have redrawn the boundaries of political districts to gain an advantage. The party in control of the state uses profiling and opinion polls to figure out which parts of the population are more likely to vote for either side. They redraw district boundaries in an attempt to ensure as many districts as possible will give them a majority vote. In other words, they group together areas in certain ways so that their own votes are maximized, or their opponents' votes are minimized. This is called gerrymandering.

The Third District of Maryland is an example of a gerrymandered district. Its odd shape was drawn to group certain voters together. The district is known as the "Praying Mantis" because of its distinctive shape.

Using maps

Using maps to predict the future is called modeling. Modeling uses data about the past to figure out what might happen in the future. One of the most useful sources of data is the **census**. The census is a national population survey that is normally held every decade. Census data allow experts to see the number of households and individuals in an area, the average age, average income, the number of children, the average educational attainment, the racial profile, or whether people live in houses, apartments, or mobile homes.

In the Real World

The Game of Planning

Modern maps can predict the future. City planners use data gathered from people through censuses and other population surveys. The data is used to create computer simulations. These simulations can show patterns of human behavior, such as how people travel to different destinations, where they like to eat out, or when they use the most water. This kind of data has also been used to create popular city-building simulation games such as SimCity. The simulations are used by planners to map how people's patterns might change over time. These "future maps" guide planners to find the best locations for schools, housing developments, transit links, hospitals, and more.

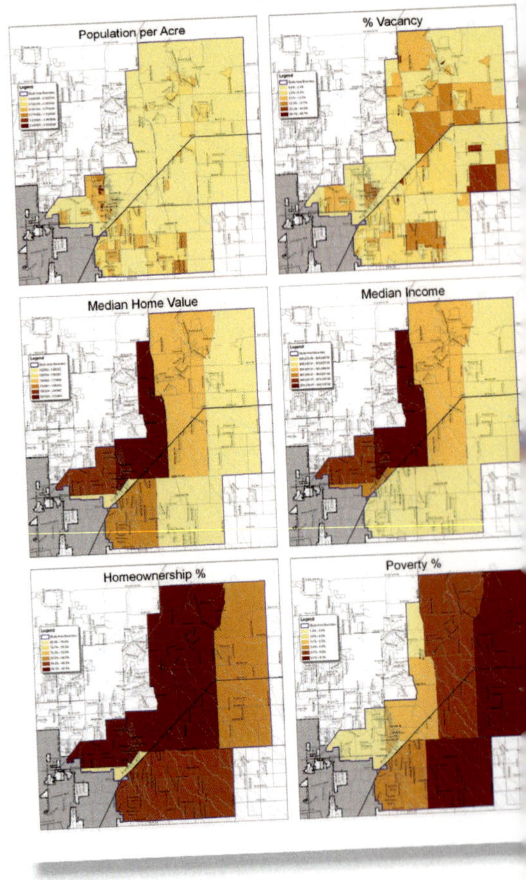

If a construction company plans to build 100 new homes in a neighborhood, modeling can show the planners the impact the new homes may have on traffic levels. Maps can show planners what intersections are likely to become busier. Maps also allow planners to see which routes children might take to school. This helps to plan how many school buses will be needed, and which routes they will take. As populations grow around the world, planners try to ensure that changing neighborhoods will have enough facilities to meet the needs of everyone who lives there.

Did You Know?

Companies that provide electricity use maps to control their networks. The maps indicate areas of high demand for power. Operators can divert power being generated from different places in the most efficient way.

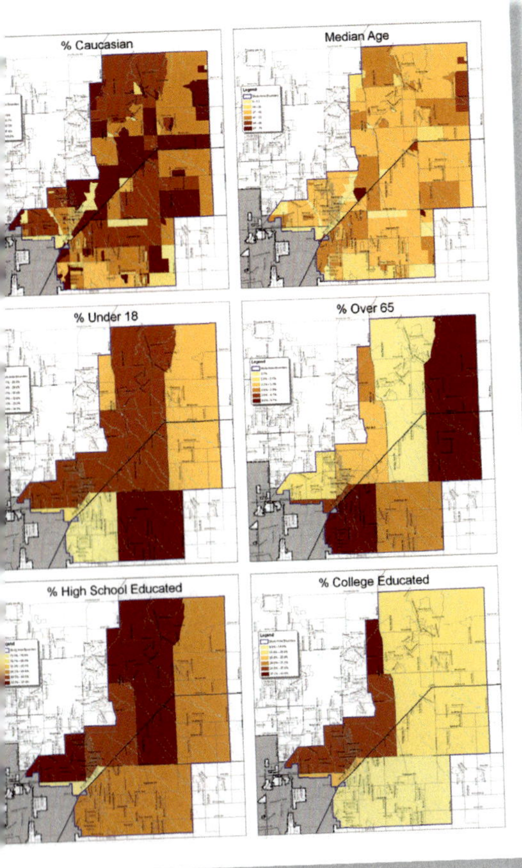

These maps of El Paso County in Colorado use census data to try to predict future population changes.

Not all modeling is concerned with human activity, however. Planners use data about creeks, streams, and wetlands to figure out the impact of construction on local water systems. A water system is the connected sources of water in an area. Planners figure out where rainwater will run if it falls onto streets rather than onto earth that soaks it up. They can see if there is a danger of pollution affecting a sensitive environmental area.

Making Data Available

With the help of modern computers, maps can be made and shared between many people. Cities can put digital maps of planned changes online for citizens to consult. Citizens can visualize the changes and see planners' models for traffic flow, school attendance, or pollution. This helps citizens engage in the planning process. If they see changes that might be harmful, they can attend public meetings or ask their elected politicians to object to the changes. They can easily share maps to raise support for their point of view.

The models used by planners take into account many types of data. The models might predict the ways people most commonly travel, such as by car, bus, or bicycle, so that they can plan for things such as public transit and bicycle lanes on busy roads.

THE FUTURE OF MAPS

Maps used to be made only by governments and big companies. Now and into the future, electronic maps can be created by anyone.

In many ways, the future of mapmaking is already here. Virtually every aspect of the world and how people live has been mapped. What is left to be developed? Some cartographers are discovering ways to map time. Google Street View has collected 360-degree photographs of streets around the world since 2007. Many city areas have been photographed more than once. Looking at these photographs reveals how cities have changed.

This NASA map shows the different rocks and minerals present on the surface of Mars.

Breakthroughs

Radical Cartogra4wqw-WQW

Some cartographers believe that maps have the power to change the ways that people think and view the world. Radical cartography is an idea that emerged in the 1960s in Detroit. Radical cartographers create maps that send certain messages or have a political or social purpose. In Detroit, radical cartographers mapped the problems of the city. One map showed the growing rat population in the city, indicating Detroit's decline into poverty. Denis Wood made a map that showed nothing but house numbers. Wood wanted to draw attention to the fact that people are often judged by where they live, or by their house numbers.

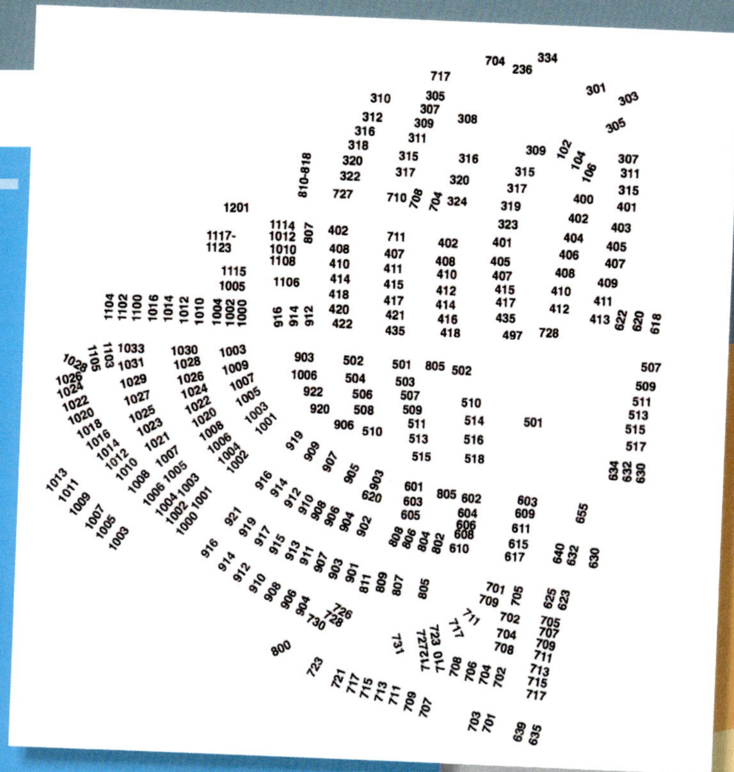

Denis Wood drew *Everything Is Numbers* by stripping out streets and buildings and showing only house numbers and their locations.

Mapping in Space

Cartographers are also looking beyond Earth. Space probes and orbiters have helped to create detailed maps of Mercury, the moon, Mars, and the moons of Jupiter and Saturn. Geologists and other scientists study these maps looking for resources such as precious rocks and minerals. They also use these maps to look for clues to how planets and moons were created. **Space observatories**, such as spacecrafts called Kepler and Gaia, orbit in space mapping nearby stars and the most distant regions of the Universe. They are helping scientists learn more about the creation of the Universe. The observatories can map the background radiation left after the **Big Bang**. Using these maps, scientists can see what the Universe may have looked like billions of years ago.

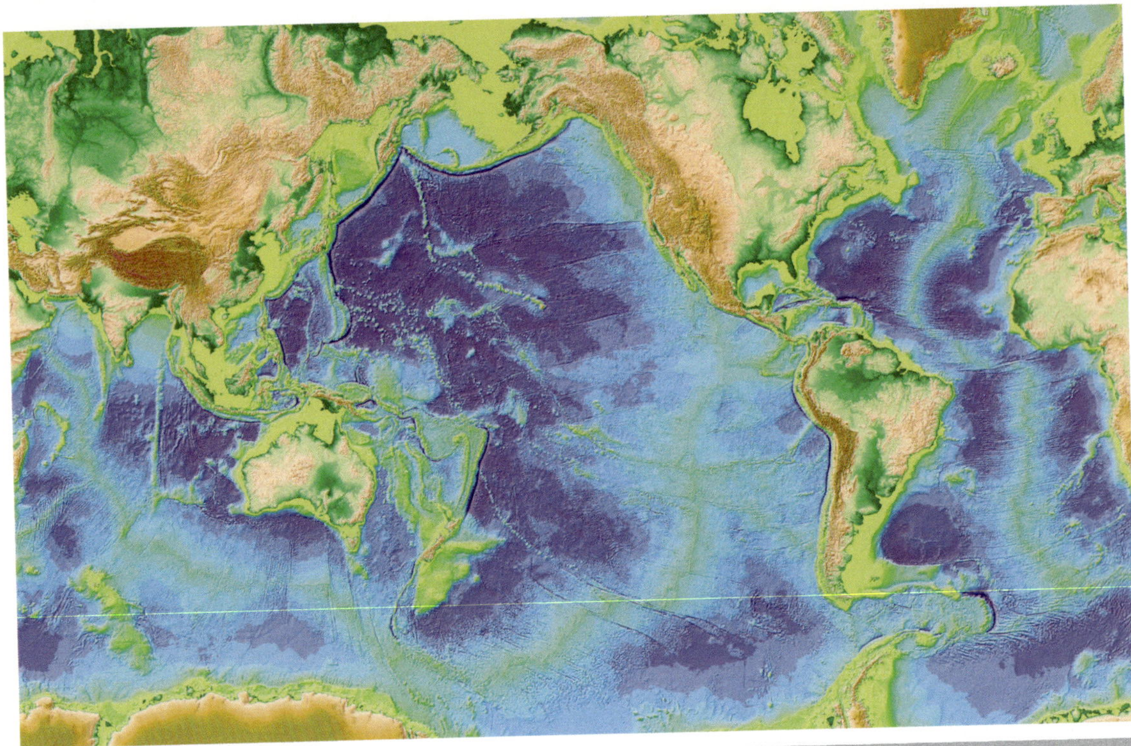

This map of the oceans shows the deepest areas as darker blue. Few of these areas have been mapped in detail.

Making Advances

Despite advances in mapping in the 2000s, cartographers still face challenges. For example, cartographers made a huge breakthrough when they mapped the trenches and ridges of the ocean floor, which revealed the shape of the Earth's **tectonic plates**. But only 5 percent of the ocean floor has been mapped. That means that up to 65 percent of the total surface of Earth remains unexplored.

Mapping the Unnoticed

All maps reflect their maker's view of what is important and what isn't. Mapmakers drawing the streets of Rio de Janeiro often overlook the favelas, or slums, around the city. This makes it more difficult to help the people living there, because information about those areas is not always recorded.

Did You Know?

One of the most exciting projects in the future of mapping is the Human Connectome Project. The scientists behind the project are trying to map the billions of connections in the human brain. They hope it will allow us to better understand the way our brains work.

Groups such as the Red Cross and Doctors Without Borders have joined together on the Missing Maps project. They work with the online mapping project OpenStreetMap to map the areas mapmakers have previously left out. When mapping our future, it seems that humans should not only look at the Universe or unexplored parts of Earth. They also need to look again at areas or people that have been overlooked. In this way, we can use maps to create a better future for all people.

These trails were left when atoms were crashed into one another and particles flew off in different directions.

In the Real World

Mapping the Unseen

As well as mapping the massive Universe and unknown areas of the ocean floor, scientists are trying to map things that are too small to see. They want to learn about the particles that make up **atoms**. Particles are the building blocks of the Universe. Everything, including you, is made up of them. Scientists use math and what they already know about atoms to calculate what these particles will be like and how to find them. Scientific facilities such as CERN in Geneva, Switzerland, use massive **particle accelerators**. These machines push small particles to close to the speed of light and crash them against other particles. Detectors monitor the crash and map the course of the fragments of the smashed particles in a cloud chamber. A cloud chamber contains dense water vapor resembling clouds, and the particles create trails of **condensation** that experts can map.

MAPS IN YOUR WORLD

New technology will make it possible for more people to create their own maps. Will these future maps be different from the kind of maps we know today?

Maps used to be expensive and difficult to make. They were only available for a few people to use. Modern technology has made maps easier to make and use. This puts far more power in the hands of ordinary people. We can work with the world around us in ways our parents could not imagine.

How do you think we will use maps in the future? Look at the different maps on these pages. They have all been created by large organizations, for specific purposes. Soon it will be possible for individuals like you to make a similar range of maps.

What kind of information would you like to learn about on a map? How could it be displayed? How would your map change the world around you? Look at the different maps on these pages to help you decide.

These maps are an image of stars from the Hubble Space Telescope (above) and a road map of part of Europe from Google Earth. Could you imagine situations where these maps might be useful?

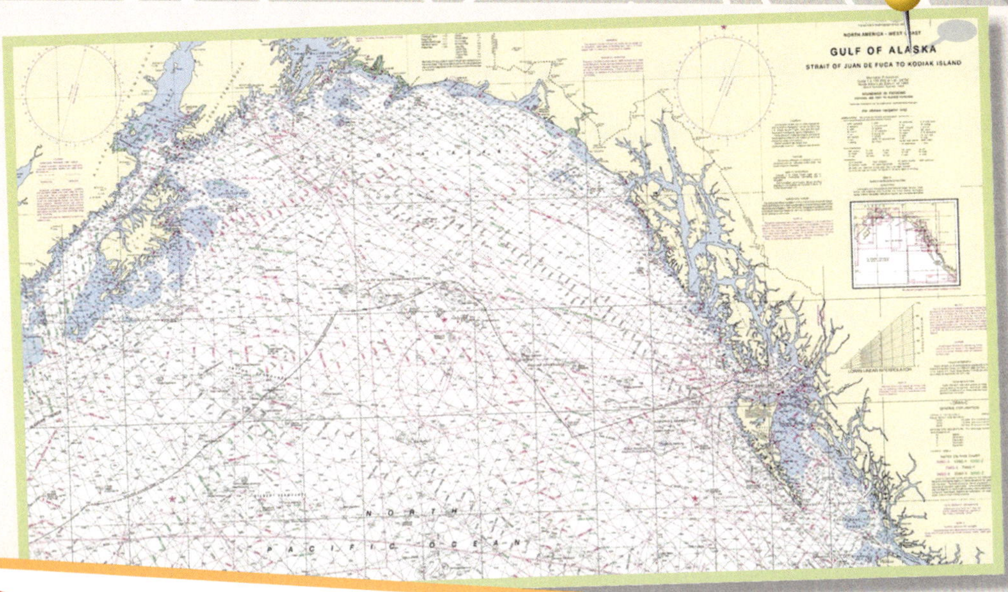

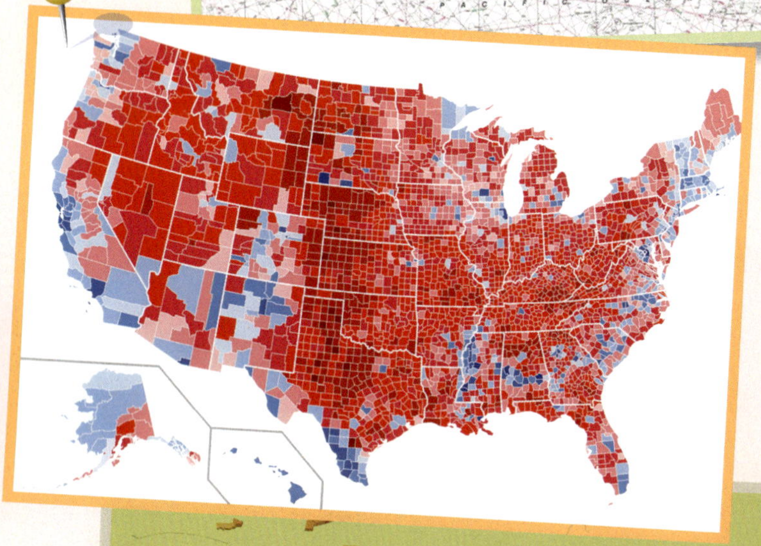

These maps are a sea chart of the Gulf of Alaska (above), a map of the results of the 2016 U.S. presidential election (left), and a 3D map of population in the Australian city of Sydney (below). Each map provides information in very different ways. What is the best way to present information on your map?

Glossary

aquifers Underground layers of rock that hold fresh water

atmosphere The layer of gas that surrounds the Earth

atoms The smallest particles of matter.

Big Bang The event in which the Universe expanded into its existence today

cartographers People who make and study maps

censorship The act of preventing information from being known

census An official count and survey of the population of a country

climate change The impact of humans on the Earth's climate

climatologists People who study the Earth's climate system

condensation Water that collects in a cool environment

customize To adapt something for a specific use or user

digital Computerized

discrimination Unfair treatment of a group of people based on their race, gender, or other qualities

Geographic Information Systems Computer programs that use a wide range of sources to generate maps

Global Positioning System A network of satellites used to provide location information

infrared A form of light that cannot be seen by the human eye

meteorologists People who study and predict the weather

NASA The National Aeronautics and Space Administration, which runs space exploration in the United States

particle accelerators Devices that crash atomic particles into one another at high speed

radiation Energy that is emitted as invisible waves

satellites Artificial bodies that orbit Earth in order to collect information

seismic Describes waves that move through the ground, as in earthquakes

sonar A device that detects sound waves as they move

space observatories Satellites equipped with a range of devices for studying outer space

spectrometers Devices that "see" nonvisible light

tectonic plates The huge plates of the Earth's crust that "float" on the molten rock beneath

triangulation A method of pinpointing a third location by using math and the distance to two known locations

ultraviolet A form of light that cannot be seen by the human eye

zoning laws Laws that divide cities into zones where certain land uses are encouraged and others barred

On the Web

www.openstreetmap.org/#map=5/51.500/-0.100
Open Street Map is a digital world map created and added to by volunteers. You can get involved and help map your local area.

www.sky-map.org
An interactive map of the Universe that allows you to explore what we are learning about objects in space.

www.missingmaps.org
A site that encourages people to map things that do not normally get mapped. Learn how to create your own maps–you may need help from an adult.

datamapper.geo.census.gov/map.html
The U.S. National Census site, where users can create their own national or local maps using information from the official census.

Books

Hirsch, Rebecca E. *Using Climate Maps*. What Do You Know About Maps? Lerner Publications, 2016.

Matteson, Adrienne. *Using Digital Maps*. Cherry Lake Publishing, 2013.

Maurer, Tracy Nelson. *Using Economic and Resource Maps*. What Do You Know About Maps? Lerner Publications, 2016.

Mizielińska, Aleksandra, and Daniel Mizieliński. *Maps*. Big Picture, 2013.

National Geographic Kids World Atlas. National Geographic Kids, 2013.

Panchyk, Richard. *Charting the World: Geography and Maps from Cave Paintings to GPS with 21 Activities*. Chicago Review, 2011.

Peetoom, Laura, and Paul Heersink. *Maps and Mapping for Canadian Kids*. Scholastic Canada, 2011.

Index